The Mind of a Millionaire

By Dr. Traci Lynn

ISBN: 978-0-9658161-0-6

Editoral Service by:
The Scribes
649 Schaffer Rd.
Marietta, GA 30060
E-mail: denisehj@msn.com

Cover Design by:
RIGHTSYDE GRAPHICS, INC.
MEDIA COMMUNICATIONS
207 Banks Station PMB 662
Fayetteville, Georgia 30214
Web site: www.rightsyde.com

Printed in the United States by Morris Publishing
3212 East Highway 30
Kearney, NE 68847
1-800-650-7888

Dedication

This Book is dedicated to my late grandmother sweet Jannie Mae Reid, whom I affectionately called "MOM". She was the True Millionaire in my life, someone who was rich with love, wisdom, and encouragement. She left me an entrepreneurial legacy to follow and she developed "The Mind of a Millionaire" in me. I also dedicate this book to my husband who provides his undying love and support, thank you CB for helping me birth this vision. And to my mother Linda Ware, who shines like an endless light of hope and vision in my life.

I love you all and thank you from the bottom of my heart.

Contents

Introduction

"For as he thinks in his heart, so is he..."
(Proverbs 23:7; THE AMPLIFIED BIBLE).

What is it that makes people millionaires? Was everyone who is a millionaire born into a wealthy family? Were they handed their wealth on a silver platter? Perhaps they all of a sudden came across an idea that propelled them into money? The truth is that people become millionaires because they think like one.

Millionaires don't think like ordinary people do. It doesn't mean that they are better than others; they are just different. If you think about it, everybody who has made any kind of impact on history has been different. Look at Abraham Lincoln, Winston Churchill, Ludwig Van Beethoven, Marion Anderson, and Wilma Rudolph. These are all people who did extraordinary things. There is something different

1

about them that allowed them to overcome all of the obstacles before them as they strove for a specific goal. Millionaires are the same way. They have tapped into some key principals that I'm going to share with you which will allow you to do the same thing.

The Bible tells us that as a man thinks in his heart, so is he. That means whatever your mind can believe you can receive. That's how we enjoy most of the conveniences of today. Before an airplane existed someone envisioned man flying. Everything we have today is the result of someone envisioning an idea and following through with it.

So how do you become a millionaire? You must think like one. If you think like a millionaire you can become a millionaire. How does a millionaire think? As we unlock the mysteries to the mind of a millionaire, we will allow the millionaire inside of you to be free. Let's enter the *mind of a millionaire* and find out.

Unlocking the Millionaire Inside

"For you created my inmost being;you knit me together in my mother's womb. I will praise you because I am fearfully and wonderfully made..." (Psalm 139:13,14; NIV).

Before you can become a millionaire you have to realize that you are already one. There is a millionaire inside of you just waiting to be free. So how do you unlock the door to your freedom? You must fulfill the vision that's been planted inside of you. What is your vision? Your vision is your divine design.

You have a divine design. When God created you He had a purpose that only you could accomplish. And He placed a desire in your heart to fulfill it. In Psalm 139 it tells us that God saw us even before we were formed in our mothers' wombs. He created us and knew the number of our days even before we were born. We were *"...fearfully and wonderfully made..."* (verse 14). And His purpose is planted as a seed in the heart of every child.

3

Dream Big

Remember how you dreamed as a child? You could see yourself doing something—providing some goods or a service that paid you well. It was a vision that just wouldn't die. It continued to get stronger and stronger; and you mulled over it for months, even years. You couldn't shake it, but as you got older it faded away because you thought it was too good to be true. What is it that you dreamed about doing as a child? Why didn't you pursue it?

A few months ago I spoke for a group of little ladies between the ages of seven and ten. I asked them, "What do you want to be when you grow up?" It was so amazing! One girl listed five occupations— a doctor, a lawyer and a cashier to start. She also wanted to work for the post office because of the benefits, and she listed something else besides those. Immediately my response was, "That's not realistic." However, one day while at home I began to think of at least three people who are doctors *and* lawyers. So you see, it was very possible for her to be a doctor, a lawyer and a cashier in the process; and maybe she can work at the post office while she's in school. It was then that I realized I had been conditioned by society to limit my vision. As you grow older you are taught not to dream big because some dreams seem impossible to fulfill. Yet children don't think that way. They haven't been conditioned by society to toss their dreams aside yet. So they're able to dream and envision themselves doing big things. They already have the mind of a millionaire because millionaires think big!

Designed for Destiny

It is your vision that will make you a millionaire—that's your way out. The Bible tells us that without a vision the people perish. So if you don't have a vision, or you're not fulfilling it, you will perish. You see, some people wonder why they can't become a millionaire while working on a job. You weren't born to work on a job. You were born to fulfill a purpose. You have a destiny and it's looking for you. Once you and your destiny meet, you are the only one who can stop it from being fulfilled. Sure there are things that get in the way to hinder you, but they can only sidetrack you. They can't stop you permanently.

God however, is the only one who can show you what your purpose is because He is the only One who knows why you were created. Once you discover and begin to pursue your purpose God will give you the anointing, strength, and power necessary to fulfill it. You see, you are an ambassador fulfilling His plan here on earth. Ambassadors are unique, set apart, different, and peculiar people. They aren't better than others, but they know that they have a purpose to fulfill. All of the forces of the country they represent back them up when they are fulfilling their purpose, and they live out the lifestyle of that country. God will do the same for you. So seek God and discover why you were created. Your gift or purpose is not your decision; it's your discovery. Pursue your vision and think big. The only way you're going to be a millionaire is to think like one. Now that we realize there is a millionaire inside each of us, let's find out how to unlock the door and let him out.

Here are seven keys that will unlock the door and free the millionaire inside. Why will I give you seven keys instead of five or nine? Seven is the number of completion and perfection.

The Tongue— Your Creative Force

"...He shall have whatsoever he saith" (Mark 11:23).

The first step in unlocking the millionaire inside of you is realizing that your tongue is a creative force. Did you know that your words are clothed with power? They have the ability to create. Proverbs 18:21 tells us that, *"Life and death are in the power of the tongue...."* That leads us to a basic biblical principle.

You Have What You Say

Take a moment to think about some of the people you know. The next time you are around them listen to the way that they talk. Then carefully observe their lives and I'm sure you'll discover that this principal is true. Your words can either make you or break you. As a motivational speaker I know the importance of watching what I say.

Now examine your own life. So what do you have right now? You have what you have been saying. We have to think about that. A lot of us have to honestly look at that and see that we are in situations right now because of our mouths. Have you been saying stuff like this? "Child I am so broke." And guess what? You probably are broke. Or, "You know I'm about to get laid off. I can't pay my car note." And then when these things happen you say, "See, I told you." You just wrote your future with your tongue. The tongue is a pen of the ready writer (Psalm 45:1). Instead why don't you say, "I'm experiencing a little cash flow problem right now, but my money is circulating and it's on its way back to me." Speak what's going to be, not what you have. If you continue to say what you have, then all you're going to have is what you've been speaking. There's no need to wallow where you are.If you wallow where you are you're going to stay there.You will have what you say.

Make sure that your conversation isn't always negative. Remember, words have power. We've been told, "Talk is cheap," and "Action speaks louder than words." Your actions speak loudly and so do your words. God is a perfect listener, so speak life.

Have you ever been around negative people? Everything that comes out of their mouths is negative. If they aren't gossiping, they're complaining or telling you about their problems. And they aren't telling you so that you can help them. They simply like to feed on negative situations. Pretty soon that negativity will start to tear you down. And you can't let that happen. So you may have to make some tough decisions concerning certain people in your life. You may have to let some of them go.

I remember a time when I had to make a decision about a particular person in my life. At the time I was married to a man who had a very good paying job in the corporate world, and Christ was not our center. To someone looking in from the outside my life looked perfect, but had I allowed myself to stay in that marriage it would have been a nightmare.

He was such a negative, critical, and controlling

person.   He also committed adultery and was verbally abusive. He constantly told me that I was nothing without him and that he made me the person that I am. We were just about to build our dream home on Main Street, and had I stayed with him I truly would have been living a *Nightmare on Main Street.*

You have to guard your mind against negative influences. You are the gatekeeper of your mind, and if you continue with certain associations they will become toxic to you. You can't allow them to be a part of your life. They can kill you and your dreams.

Cleanse Your Tongue

It's up to you to feed your mind positive food. Your mind needs food just like your body needs food. You must keep your mind clean and pure. So cleanse your tongue. Do what you have to do. Go to church; listen to positive tapes. Start repeating positive affirmations. Say what the Bible says about you and your situations. Begin to tell yourself, "I am fearfully and wonderfully made. I am successful. "

And you are successful because you took a step towards achieving your goal by purchasing and reading this book. *You put your money where your mouth is.* You're a millionaire in the making. So continue to build yourself up with positive words. Remember, words are seeds. And whatever words you allow to be planted in your mind will grow. They will affect what you believe and achieve. After all, if you believe that you can, you will; but if you believe that you can't, you won't. Ninety percent of what you believe is what you are going to have.

Now that you've seen the power of words you can see how they affect your vision. So many times our visions never have the chance to be born because someone else's negative words have killed them in the womb. We'll go into more detail about that later. However, suppose that you are already making positive affirmations but they are not successful. You began a business that you thought you could enjoy working at and you were sure that you could do it well. Somehow it just doesn't seem to be working out. By now you are probably thinking, *What am I doing wrong?* The answer to that question brings me to my next step—Till Your Own Land.

Till Your Own Land

"He that tilleth his land shall have plenty of bread...."
(Proverbs 28:19).

Have you ever decided to enter a moneymaking venture just because someone else did it and it worked for him or her? Well just because it worked for that person doesn't mean that it will work for you, unless of course it is your purpose. Let me give you an example of what I mean. My cousin had a nail salon and I watched her make $3000 in one Saturday. Naturally, being the entrepreneur that I am, I decided that if she could make that much money in one day, so could I. I however, was thinking on a much larger scale. I think big—like a millionaire. I knew that it would take a minimum of twenty thousand dollars a week to make me a millionaire. And she was only doing $3000 a day; so I had to multiply her output. I hired ten women to go into hair salons and do nails. I set them up with stations, bought them all of the products, and business was going great. It was phenomenal and I was doubling what she was doing! Three months later I was out of business and broke. What happened?

Fulfilling Purpose

Well first of all, I didn't like the smell of the products. And secondly, I didn't have any knowledge of that business. I had a business attitude but no business aptitude. I could have gone to school and learned that business only; several people do. Even if I had gone to school however, it would not have worked. Aptitude was only half of the problem. The other half of the problem is that I was tilling my cousin's land. I know at least seven people who started nail salons because of my cousin's and theirs didn't work either. We were trying to live her vision, not our own. That's what happens with a lot of us. We end up tilling someone else's land, trying to live his or her dreams. Some of us even spend time in school trying to obtain knowledge in a specific area so that we can succeed, but it is not our vision. We follow the market trends instead or our destinies, but if we listen to them every one in here would have a job in computers. Then we would probably end up unfulfilled and stuck in occupations that barely pay the bills because God didn't design all of us to work with computers.

I tilled several lots of land before I discovered my purpose. I actually had five businesses before my jewelry business succeeded. At age 15 I found myself doing all of my classmates' hair. I worked from a vacant apartment that my mother owned. That helped me get into college. I was also able to earn extra money in college by doing hair. Then by age 19 I founded the first chapter of a national sorority on my college campus. I was told that it couldn't be done, but I did it. Then I went on at age 21 to begin **Traci's Unique Paraphernalia Boutique.** Someone had to supply the sorority with the paraphernalia. Others were concerned that I wouldn't be able to keep up my grades and do all of this at the same time; but I kept up my grades and did it all. Even though these ventures succeeded, I couldn't stay there. They were just steps along the pathway to my destiny. They were experiences that helped make me the person I am today.

When I got married another business venture began. I had a big wedding. I liked planning *my* wedding. As a matter of fact, I had so much fun that I decided to go into business planning weddings. I took out an ad in the Yellow Pages. The name of the business was "A Bride's Dream." It started with the letter "A" so it was the first name in the telephone book. I had people calling me, wanting my service, but I only wanted to take on one client at a time. When it was all said and done, I made two dollars and twenty-five cents an hour. I was not going to be a millionaire in that business. What made it even worse was that I realized I didn't even like it because the bride got on my last nerve! It's funny how you do something when you think money is involved, even though you realize you really don't like it.

When you discover your purpose however, your work will be a joy because where there is purpose there is joy. So how do you discover your own purpose? There is a saying that goes, "Because I love what I do, I would do it for free; but because I do it so well, people will pay me for it." What is it that you've always loved doing but others have tried to talk you out of? That's probably it. You've probably had people tell you, "Don't go into business doing that. I tried it and it didn't work for me." Well it probably didn't work for that person because it wasn't his or her purpose. You won't have to worry about their failures, because if the business is for you it will work for you. You'll make money with it because wherever your vision is God will give the provision. He'll open up doors for you and provide everything that you need, because you will be fulfilling His vision for your life. Johann Goethe said, "Whatever you can do or dream you can begin it! For boldness has genius, power and magic in it. Begin it now!"

Making the God—Connection

The key word here however, is God. As I mentioned in chapter two, your vision must come from Him. Proverbs 29:18 says, *"Where there is no vision* (no redemptive revelation of God) *the people perish."* You must have His mind in order to accomplish your purpose because only He can tell you your reason for existing. Otherwise you only have ninety percent of the puzzle. And without that last ten percent you have no puzzle. So whose mind do you have? Whose dreams are you pursuing? Are they yours?

When I graduated from High School I went to college and studied medicine because throughout my life my mother instilled in me the desire to become a doctor. Yet when I began my internship I was always fainting because I couldn't stand the sight of blood or needles. After talking to some counselors, I realized that my strengths were in business. So I had to make a decision. Was I going to continue on the medical path and attempt to live out a purpose that wasn't mine to fulfill? Or was I going to make a change and do something that I liked and could do well? I decided to pursue a degree in business even though my mother didn't like it. It wasn't an easy choice for me because my mother has always been a strong influence in my life. Now I have a speaking business, a national television ministry, and own several franchises. I'm successful because I'm walking in purpose. I finally began tilling my own land.

Once you've started tilling your own land you've only begun fulfilling your destiny. But there are several things that you need to be aware of if you are going to be successful and fulfill your destiny. Fear is one of them. Overcoming fear is the next key to unlocking the millionaire inside of you.

Overcoming Fear

*"For God hath not given us the spirit of fear;
but of power..." (2 Timothy 1:7).*

The third step to thinking like a millionaire is overcoming fear. Do you know what *fear* is? *Fear* is **F**alse **E**ducation **A**ppearing **R**eal. Fear cripples your faith and places it in a wheelchair because your trust is in the wrong information. You see your faith is the thing that will take you from one place to another. But how can you get around when you cripple that one thing that can help you succeed? Fear cripples faith. It holds you back. We as adults are fearful of so many different things. But have you ever watched children? They are so robust and have such a thirst for life that they aren't afraid of anything.

I have a stepdaughter, Natalie, and she isn't scared of anything. Now I, on the other hand, am afraid of bugs. That's not good because we live in the woods. One evening my mother and I were outside grilling and it began to get dark. Of course when it gets dark the bugs come out and gather around the light. So the bugs began to come out but there was this one big bug that flew and walked; it flew and walked. As that bug started coming toward us we began running and screaming. We ran into the house and closed the door. Well guess what got in? That huge bug that flew and walked got into the house and we were terrified. Now I knew that Natalie, who was ten at the time, wasn't afraid of bugs. So I screamed for her in a loud voice, "Natalie, Natalie!"

I had just put her in the bathtub. She came running down the stairs with the towel wrapped around her, dripping wet and wondering what was wrong. I said, "Get that bug!" She went over to it, looked at it, picked it up by the wings and held it in my face. Then she said, "You're scared of this? I can't believe you did all that yelling and screaming for this. It's only a grasshopper. It can't even bite you." Then I thought about it. We are running from grasshoppers—things that we can stomp with our feet. Those are the fears that cripple us.

Golden Handcuffs

What kind of fears are you allowing to cripple you? Most of us don't become millionaires because of the job. Yes we let the **J-O-B** keep us from fulfilling our purposes. It keeps us just over broke. We don't make enough money to pay our bills, but at least we get a steady paycheck. We are held up by those golden handcuffs—retirement, health care, dental and life insurance. They give us security, but they hold us to the job. Then most people find themselves saying, "They pay me just enough not to quit, and I'm going to do just enough not to get fired." So they don't give it their all because it's just a JOB to them. It's not their purpose. There's no joy in it—no fulfillment.

My question to you is this. Who told you that you couldn't have those benefits as an entrepreneur? Some of your jobs offer you profit sharing. If you're an entrepreneur you can have profit sharing. Would you prefer to get five percent of the profit or a hundred percent? As for dental and health care benefits, you can buy those benefits. My benefits don't cost me anymore now than they did when I left my job. I think I was twenty-five when I left my job and I've never been back since then. I still pay the same amount in benefits. The difference now is that *I* say what doctor I want to see, not *them.* It's good to be in that position. The choice is mine. These are the things that hold us back, and it's intimidation. Break free from those golden handcuffs.

The Inner Me—Enemy

Often we allow fear to keep us from doing what is necessary to become a millionaire. But where is that voice coming from that's talking to us, telling us to stay on the JOB? If you stop and think about it, no one is standing over you whispering in your ear and telling you to remain on the job. It is the inner voice, the inner me—enemy. That inner voice has become the enemy because it keeps you from moving ahead. You see, sometimes we talk ourselves out of the things that God has for us because of fear. We're afraid to come out of our comfort zones and try something different, something new. That inner me—

enemy is telling you to stay where it is safe and depend on that paycheck. Your faith however, shouldn't be in the paycheck but in God as your source. After all, we walk by faith and not by sight. So you must be careful not to allow the inner me— enemy to prevent you from fulfilling your destiny.

The battlefield is in the mind. It is there that you must defeat fear. Fear will tell you that you need to go to school to get another degree before you can pursue your vision. And another degree is all right, but I was a millionaire before my doctorate. I like what Dr. Myles Munroe says, "When fish are born do they go to swimming school or are fish born with the swim in them?" You and I are born with the basics to fulfill our purpose; education should serve to enhance what's there naturally. You can't go back to get more education because of fear and intimidation. You have to go for the right reasons. I know people who are professional students. They have been in school for ten or fifteen years. They have business plans but haven't done anything with them. Suppose you do go back to school and get all of this education. Are you willing to put it to use?

You have got to be confident that you have what it takes to be successful. Encourage yourself. Stroke yourself sometimes. It is also important to build a support system of people who encourage you too, but we'll discuss more of this in the next chapter. Replace that fear with faith. Tell yourself that you can make it if you pursue your purpose. Don't let the inner me continue to be the enemy.

The Pimp and the Prostitute

A job will not only keep you in handcuffs and make your inner me your enemy, it will cause you to lose faith in yourself and prostitute your gifts. Think about it. The pimp tells the prostitute how much she will get paid, what her job description is, and what hours she will work. While this is going on, the pimp makes a profit off of the prostitute. A job does the same thing. It tells you how much they think you are worth, how much they plan on paying you, and when and how you will work. It also gives you an evaluation and places a value on your performance—excellent, average, below average, and poor. And if you're not careful you'll believe it. Don't allow your job to cause you to prostitute your talents. Discover and fulfill your divine purpose.

You know, one day I was talking with a lady who had gotten news that her job was laying people off. She had been working there for 25 years. She became so upset by the thought of being laid off that she responded by saying, "I don't know what I'm going to do if they lay me off. I've done this all my life and this is all I know." I realized then that this woman had become everything that her employer wanted from her, but she never tried to find out what her purpose was. Don't give so much of yourself to your employer that you have nothing left for you. If you're working eight hours a day on the job and when you get home you don't have enough time or energy to do some things for yourself, you're giving too much to your employer. Seek God and discover your purpose. Become pregnant with a vision and pursue it.

Carrying the Baby—Abortion, Miscarriage, and Adoption

Your vision is your baby. Once you become

pregnant with the vision, give birth to the baby and raise it. Don't allow fear to come in and steal the baby from you. Fear is one of the enemy's tactics. It will cause you to do three things to your vision. It will cause you to abort your vision, have a miscarriage, or let someone else fulfill your vision once you've given birth to it.

If you're not careful, once you are pregnant with the vision, fear will tell you that you can't do anything with that vision. It will say, "You'll never be successful at it." Fear will scream, "Abort now!" But you can't even take your mind there, or you'll lose the vision before it even begins to grow.

Then there are some of you whose visions will grow. You'll begin to nurture the vision just like a baby is nourished in the mother's womb, and things will flow well. Once you get close to delivery time in the sixth or seventh month however, if you aren't careful fear of failure will grip you. You'll say, "Oh my God, I am not going to be able to do this. I thought I could handle it." You'll begin looking at those around you who've failed and think, *If she failed at it, I'm going to be the laughing stock of everybody. I'm going to fail.* After worrying yourself about it you'll say, "Forget it," and you'll miscarry the baby.

Then there are those of you who will go all the way through. You'll have a healthy pregnancy and deliver a healthy baby. And you'll let everybody around you start raising the baby. They'll tell you what to do and how it should be done. Soon enough you'll get tired of it, become insecure and say, "Here, you take the baby." And you give away your vision—the baby you nurtured and delivered. Now you're sitting back watching someone else do your thing. Fear will do that to your vision. So you must rise above fear or you'll find yourself going around the same mountain over and over again just like the Israelites did when they left the land of Egypt. They had the opportunity to enter the Promised Land but allowed fear to keep them out. They said that *they* were like grasshoppers in the eyes of the giants of that land. Instead of enjoying the benefits that had been promised to them, they spent forty years in the wilderness. And it was all because they refused to think in faith. They chose to yield to fear.

Get Out of the Wilderness

"...Let us go up at once, and possess it; for we are well able to overcome it" (Numbers 13:30).

The fourth key to thinking like a millionaire is leaving the wilderness mentality behind. The wilderness is the period of time you spend building your vision without seeing the results. Every vision will have a wilderness. There is always trouble before deliverance, but how long you stay in the wilderness is up to you.

The Evil Report

In the last chapter I mentioned the children of Israel. If you're familiar with the story about the Israelites, you know that they left Egypt with a wilderness mentality. God told them prepare to go into the Promised Land; instead they sent twelve spies in to check out the land. Ten of the spies returned with an evil report saying, "We can't do it. The giants are there." Even though they came back with a bunch of grapes so big that it had to be put on a staff and carried by two men, they didn't believe that they could possess the land. Joshua and Caleb however, returned with a good report. They knew that Israel was well able to overcome the enemy. But because the Israelites believed the evil report God punished that generation. He had them walk around in the wilderness for forty years when they should have crossed the wilderness in forty days. Joshua, Caleb and their families were the only ones in that generation who inhabited the Promised Land. All of the other people from the older generation died before the new generation could enter the Promised Land.

Sometimes your wilderness mentality can be generational too. Everyone else in your family could have been poor, but that shouldn't stop you from becoming a millionaire and possessing your destiny. You can't let the past generations or the giants stop you. If God gave you a vision then you can possess it. The choice is yours.

You must remember that every vision goes through a wilderness, but you don't have to stay there for forty years. You need to go through something in order to get something. You also have to be able to ignore the evil reports, stand up in the midst of your wilderness and say, "I am well able to overcome."

Just Hang in There

I remember when I decided to do something that I was passionate about—my jewelry. I went out into the neighborhood and began handing out flyers at the train station. This was my wilderness because I was trying to build something. Do you know what people said to me as I was handing out those flyers? "Get a real job." People can be cruel. Do you know that? They would snatch my flyer out of my hand and throw it in the garbage can right in front of me. Some of the people whom I graduated from high school with would pass by and say, "Traci, I heard that you were doing bad, but I didn't know that you were doing this bad." And I had to keep smiling and take it because I was in my wilderness. I hadn't made any money yet. I could have just said, "I don't need this. Forget it!" Then I could have gone back to working on a job like those people were doing.

As I watched them throw my flyers in the garbage can I felt so low. To them I wasn't anybody, but I was always somebody to me. I had to endure that and keep going. I kept handing out those flyers because I knew that my wilderness wouldn't last forever. Then one day, several months later, I had a meeting with some people in that section of the city near the train station where I used to hand out my flyers. And I saw some of those same people getting on the train. Of course I drove up in my Lexus Coupe and blew my horn, "Beep, beep! It's me the flyer girl. How are you all doing? Are you still at that *job?* It's the flyer girl with the Lexus Coupe." You see you've got to understand your own wilderness and know that you're coming out of it. You can't let what goes on in the wilderness discourage you and keep you from fulfilling your vision and purpose.

Coming Soon

Have you ever seen a construction site? The land is usually covered with rocks, bottles, dirt, trash, some stubble, and a bit of dead grass. The owners have broken ground and placed a big sign with a picture on it of what the building is going to look like when it has been completed. The sign says, "Coming Soon." Right now you may be like that construction site. You have a vision of what you want to be, but all the average person can see is stubble and grass. They don't have your vision. They can't see what God has in store for you. One thing you have to remember is that no one knows your vision but you and God. So you can't let other people's opinion of you become your reality. You are in charge of how you think and feel. Don't let people steal your dreams because they can't see your vision. That's all right if all others can see is stubble and grass because there is a banner on your forehead right now saying, "Coming Soon." And no matter how tough it gets in your wilderness, you must always remember that you are *coming soon.*

While speaking at seminars, I've had people ask

me how my business became successful because they didn't want to make the same mistakes that I've made. The truth is that no matter how well you plan it's not going to go perfectly; the wilderness is unavoidable. You can't avoid all of the pitfalls and quicksand. Unexpected situations often arise. However, you must be able to regroup and keep stepping. Sometimes your best ideas come from those times when you're in the wilderness. Adversity reveals genius; prosperity conceals it. You'll make it if you keep working at it. The question is, "Can you endure?"

Link Up with Winners

It's important to have positive, supportive people in your life. You need that encouragement as you're building your vision. Hook up with people who aren't users leeches, or those who simply agree with you in order to get on your good side. You have to surround yourself with people of like minds, people who are on their way up, not people who have the wilderness mentality. I remember when I decided to purchase my Lexus Coupe there were people in my family who said, "Don't get that kind of car. I could never afford it." They would tell me what they couldn't do as if I had the same mind that they do. They were still in the wilderness. But I couldn't listen to that. You see I had to abandon that old way of thinking.

You have to link up with people who have the same mind as you. How can someone who doesn't even have the faith to make $50,000 a year believe that you can make one million dollars a year? If they can't believe it for themselves they can't believe it for you. Sometimes you are going to have to make some tough choices. You're going to have to let go of some people in your life. You will need to give and take support from people of a like mind. Whatever you do, you don't want to have a wilderness mentality or you'll stay in the wilderness. Remember, you are only there for a season.

I had to develop a group of people I call my *front row*. My *front row* is made up of people whom I can confide in and exchange support with. They are people like my husband, my grandmother, my mother, and two close friends. Everybody can't be a front row member. When I go to speaking engagements the front row is my support system. Everyone else is in the bleachers. Their opinion doesn't have as powerful an impact on my life.

You need to get yourself a *front row* too. Get a support system of people who will be honest with you and encourage you. You need people who will tell you, "You need to go back this way. You're going off a little bit too far on this end. Don't get caught up over there." See that's what a true friend will do. Once you have developed your support group you will begin to realize a very important fact. And that brings me to the next step in the process of having the mind of a millionaire.

You Are the Key

"...Write the vision, and make it plain upon tables,
that he may run that readeth it" (Habakkuk 2:2).

The next step to developing the mind of a millionaire is realizing that the key to reaching your goal is within you. You will have to visualize yourself going places before anyone else can. That's faith. And faith is the solid foundation that you will need to give birth to your vision. You must know that there is a millionaire inside of you just waiting to burst forth. You need to think like a millionaire. Do you have coach mentality or first class mentality? Millionaires have first class mentality. Often we want to say that we have first class mentality, but when it comes down to it, is it true? What side of the street do you see yourself living on?

On a recent flight, I was sitting in coach before that flight took off and a flight attendant came to me out of nowhere and said, "Ma'am would you like to sit in

36

first class." I said "What?" He said again "Would you like to sit in first class". I said, "Who sent you?" He said "Ma'am I'm only going to ask you one more time, do you want to sit in first class?" I said finally, "Yes sir I do!" Now that was the favor of God. Later during the flight, I asked him "Why did you ask me to sit in first class, he said "because you looked like you belong here." So you know what that means, you have to FAKE IT TILL YOU MAKE IT!

Develop A Plan

You may have already posted your sign saying, "Coming Soon," but you have to visualize what you want and develop a plan to achieve it. Find out what it takes to accomplish your goal. Prepare for it. Without a plan—a blueprint—your house might have one wall too long and the other one too short. The roof might not fit properly. You have to sit down and calculate before you can build. So get a picture of what you want to build. See yourself doing that thing. The Bible tells us to count the cost, and write the vision and make it plain so that you can see it and run with it. You need to keep a blueprint of your vision before you so that you will be able to recognize your opportunities to achieve the vision when they are presented to you. Your mind is a powerful tool. That's how I got featured in *Essence* magazine.

I went on a trip to Universal Studios in Florida earlier that year. While I was there I took one of those fun pictures that will let you take a picture of yourself on the cover of any magazine that you want to. So I took a picture of myself on the cover of *Essence.* The very next month I heard that Susan Taylor, the Editor-n-Chief of *Essence,* was coming to town and this was my opportunity to meet her. So I bought a ticket and went to the luncheon.

When I met her I introduced myself. I told her that I was a motivational speaker who had a story to tell and I wanted to be featured in *Essence.* I said, " You don't have to be 50 to live your dreams. You can be 21, 22, or 29." She said, "Sounds great. Send me your information." So I gathered together a press kit and mailed it to her office. A couple of days later I called her office for a follow-up and spoke to Deborah, her assistant. I said, "Did you get my press kit?" She requested that I send it again.

So I sent the press kit again. I had to deal with a lot of bureaucracy, so I asked myself the question, "How badly do you want to be in *Essence?*" After a few more follow-up phone calls and press kits, I heard that Susan would be back in my city in two months for a book signing. I went to the book signing and was the last person in line for the first session.

I said, "Susan, do you remember me?" She said, "Vaguely." I told her that she liked my story and said that I could be in *Essence* magazine. She asked me if I had my information with me. Now how hungry was I? I didn't even have my information with me. So I told her that I would come back because I had a thousand independent consultants and I'm going to buy some books for them. She said, "You're going to come back and buy a thousand books?" I said, "No, no, no, but I think I'm going to come back and get some books." She said, "You're going to come back and get 50 books?" I said, "Uh!" Now 50 times $14.95 is no small piece of change, but you know what? I bought those 50 books because I was hungry to be in *Essence* magazine.

I stood in line for three hours. I made up a list of people for Susan to autograph those books to. While she was signing those books I had my press kit. Somebody was massaging her back and I thought, *I've got her now.* I presented my press kit to her and she said, "All right, are you ready?"

I said, "Ready for what?"

She said, "For what's about to happen. You will be featured in the September issue of *Essence* magazine, and people will be calling you and writing to you by the thousands."

I said, "Yes I am."

If I had never seen myself featured in Essence magazine, I would never have seen my vision come to reality. You have to keep your vision before your eyes and cultivate your vision.

Cultivate Your Vision

When my husband, CB, and I decided to sell the house we were living in we went around taking pictures of the kind of home we wanted. We went to other houses that were really big—four thousand square feet and up. They were $500,000 homes. At that time I thought, *this is not my next house, but I'm going to look at it anyway.* So we went around in this particular neighborhood and found a house that my husband and I really liked. I had CB take a picture of me posing at the front door of one house. And to keep the neighbors from becoming suspicious and calling the police, I ran around back really quickly and had him take a picture of me there too. (The owners were probably off on a vacation somewhere in Florida.) We hung those pictures on our mirror so that we could look at them and envision our dream home. The funny thing about it was that whenever someone came to view the house that we were trying to sell, they wanted to buy the house in the picture instead.

The house in the picture was not the one we were trying to buy. At that time, we didn't have faith for a $500,000 house. The house we were buying was a $250,000 home. We were just about ready to close on it when we found a $500,000 house just like the one in the picture. It was just like the one we had envisioned ourselves living in. Now our natural minds said, "You must be crazy. You can't get this right now. What about the expenses involved in keeping up the property?" Lo and behold, eight months later, we moved into that $500,000 home. We were only able to move into that home because we saw ourselves there by faith. If we hadn't taken the pictures we would have never been able to visualize ourselves living in a $500,000 home. That picture became the blueprint for our vision. We received it because we saw ourselves in it by faith, before we saw ourselves living in it in the natural.

Prepare for Delivery

Once you can visualize your goal, prepare to deliver your baby. If my husband and I weren't prepared we would have missed our opportunity to buy that house. We had to be ready to seize the opportunity that presented itself to us. And you must do the same. Otherwise you'll find yourself sitting in coach instead of first class.

Speaking of opportunities, I can recall when I first had the opportunity to introduce myself to Les Brown. I flew out to his "Speaking for Living" seminar in Chicago. He was scheduled to be closer to my home in New York later that year, but I couldn't wait that long. I wanted to meet him as soon as possible. I envisioned that we would be working together. During the seminar he gave the participants a chance to introduce themselves. There was my opportunity to make my impression. So I boldly stood up and introduced myself. I told him that I was in the jewelry business and was very successful at what I did. I made it quite clear that I was there to meet him. I wanted him to see me because I had a vision that we would work together. I could see after I introduced myself that I had peaked Les' interest. That was only the beginning however, and I was not prepared for the next step.

We were seated at tables in groups of eight, and

we all had to give mini-presentations at our tables. I sized up the competition at my table. Everyone was there for different reasons. Some were there to be a part of Les Brown's new speaking guild, others weren't. So when I gave my presentation I wasn't as forceful or as powerful as I was when I spoke in front of Les. We were only talking to the people at the table. So I told myself, "It's no big deal." I didn't realize however, that each table was going to pick a winner who would compete with the other tables' winners by giving a speech right in front of Les. He, in turn, would pick a winner from that competition and reward that person with the Golden Microphone Award.

Unwittingly, I was a little laid back in my presentation. Another lady at my table however, was not. When she gave her presentation she let us have it! She was dynamic, awesome. She was everything that I should have been. I lost the competition at my table by three points and came in second place. I did not make it to the final round. Had I given it my all I may have won, because the lady from my table was the grand winner of the "Golden Microphone Award." I didn't take full advantage of the opportunities presented to me. I was afraid that I had missed an opportunity to become a part of Les's team because I didn't give my best. Sometimes we do the same thing when it comes to pursuing our purposes. We don't take the opportunities that are presented to us seriously, and we end up missing the opportunity to walk through an open door.

Everything wasn't lost though. As Les was signing autographs he wrote on my book, "You've got the gift." He did see the ability for me to be a motivational speaker when I gave my first presentation. I hadn't failed after all. To make a long story short, I went back to Philadelphia, and a month later I was opening for Les Brown. I was destined to work with him because that was my vision. Remember, when you are pursuing your vision God provides what you need. He worked everything out after all.

Quit Taking It Personally

As you prepare to take advantage of the many

opportunities that come your way, be careful not to get an attitude or give up if an opportunity doesn't work out the way you thought it would. I have a recipe that will help you to remember to keep smiling and have a pleasant attitude no matter what the outcome. Take a Q-tip and place it on a 5x7 card. Then write on it, "Q-Tip." You know what that stands for? Quit taking it personally. We take too many things personally, and as we do the distress of those situations comes out in the words we speak. If you feel down because of something that happened, you'll continue to talk about those situations and you will have what you say. So don't sweat the small stuff.

If things don't go the way you wanted them to, get over it. Cry if you have to, but take it as a lesson learned and keep going. See it as a challenge that you had to be stretched to meet, and continue on to the next step. It simply may not be the right time for your idea, but that doesn't mean that there is something wrong with the idea itself. If it's for you nothing will stop you from getting it.

I can remember when I wanted to do a motivational radio talk show on a local station here in

Philadelphia. Now I had a choice; I could either pay for the time or convince the station manager that he should let me do it for free. I chose the second option. I called the station several times and spoke to the station manager. Unfortunately, he decided that he didn't want to take the station in that direction at the time. I continued to call regularly. I was patient and courteous. I didn't give up or become indignant. Later on that year Les Brown came to town and did a three-hour talk show at that same station. During the show the station phones lit up with calls from interested listeners. So I took advantage of the opportunity to talk to the station manager once again about letting me do this same type of talk show. This time he was ready and I was able to get on at that station.

Now had I become indignant or nasty on the telephone when I spoke with him earlier, I would have closed my door to the opportunity to speak with him when Les came to town. So remember to keep a pleasant attitude when you're dealing with people. Continue to be patient. On the other hand, had Les Brown not come to town I may have never gotten on at that station. Sometimes, who you know will walk you through an open door faster than what you know. Regardless of how I got on, God opened the door for me.

Destined to Win

There are times when opportunities will present themselves to you, and they look like they're for you. You think that your ship has really come in. But when you get right upon it you see that it's nothing but an old barge carrying scrap metal. Take for instance the time when a billion-dollar infomercial company was interested in my jewelry. I was invited to attend one of their board meetings. So I did. The president was impressed and as he was walking out of the meeting he told the vice president, "I want this! Work with her." Everything looked promising. The deal however, also required that I give up a lot of control during a crucial stage in my business and I felt a little uneasy about that. I consulted my husband and mother about it and they told me to make the decision that I felt comfortable with. I always pray, "Thy will be done, Lord." And I know that God honors that prayer. So the board and I worked on the proposal for a few weeks and tried to get everything together. Then one day just as the deal was about to go through, I received a call saying that the company was going to pass on it.

I was a little disappointed but not devastated. I realized that God had intervened. He had something better for me. Remember, nothing just happens; things happen just and within twelve months, that billion-dollar infomercial company went out of Business. No, things don't always work out the way you think they will. Sometimes you think an opportunity is one thing, but it's another. So that deal didn't go through, but a year later I began marketing my own jewelry on television, and I had total control.

Remember, all things work together for your good because you are a winner. You were a winner before you were born. Did you know that of all the sperm sent to fertilize your egg only one could do it, and it had to be the fastest sperm? So the sperm that fertilized your egg was a winner, and so are you. You were created to win, so expect it.

Faith

"For we walk by faith, not by sight"
(2 Corinthians 5:7).

Faith will help you maintain an attitude of expectancy. Even though you are destined to win, the steps that you must climb in the process of becoming a millionaire can be challenging. With faith however, you can win. What is faith? Faith is the substance of what you're hoping for, and the evidence of what you are going after.

Faith is what you hold on to while you're going through the wilderness. It helps you to see every inch, every detail of your vision so that you will know what your baby is supposed to look like. It will allow you to raise the sign that says, "Coming Soon." Faith will help you step outside of your comfort zone and go for your dream. It will give you the confidence to believe in yourself even when others don't, and the determination to keep going when others quit. Faith is the foundation that carries your vision from conception to delivery. It will keep you each step of the way and lead you to places you've only dreamed of going.

Step by Step

Faith is what got me into my house. I certainly didn't get there because of what I had in my bank account. If you've ever bought a house you know how complicated the process can be. They go back seven years when they check your credit, and I had some blemishes on my record. After all, when I went to college I had several credit cards. And as a college student, I just didn't handle my finances very wisely. Today things are different. However, when you are buying a house, the mortgage company considers your past as well as your present. Regardless of what my credit history or my financial statement said, we got the house. We stood in faith because we had a vision. We took pictures of ourselves in front of a house just like the house we wanted to live in. When the opportunity presented itself to purchase the kind of house we had envisioned ourselves living in, we seized it. Our finances said that we could only afford a $250,000 home, but faith gave us something bigger and better. Despite our financial statements we are living in that house. It all happened by faith.

Faith will not only help you to grasp your vision, it will help you to keep it. The first month after we got the house fear tried to enter my heart, but it couldn't win. When fear tried to enter I had to build myself back up in faith. You see, when you are walking in God's purpose you don't have to wonder how you are going to maintain what He has given you. There's no need to fear losing what He's given you or not knowing what to do with it because everything will be revealed to you as you go. That's what walking in faith is all about. When God has given you the vision, He will provide.

Not only will He provide, He will put His anointing upon it. There is a difference between a gift and the anointing on a gift. Anybody can have a gift and do fine with it. When you have the anointing that means that God is with you. And when God is with you who can be against you? There's no reason to fear. Things will begin falling in place as He opens doors for you.

You must also be careful not to focus on the size of the open door. There are times when something small comes along and it springboards you to the next level. Don't despise small beginnings. Continue to walk by faith and one step will lead you to another. When I began selling my jewelry I never considered motivational speaking. I never aspired to do this as a little girl; I didn't know anything about it. Yet I love speaking and I do it passionately. I don't have any training as a speaker, but I don't need it because speaking is my gift—my purpose, my destiny. I'm doing several things now that I hadn't even considered doing when I started my jewelry because I'm following God's lead. Often people have asked me, "How can you run four successful businesses? I can barely run one." The answer is, "I am fulfilling my purpose. This is what I was created to do." I do them successfully because of God's anointing on my life. He has led me into each area that I'm involved in.

Overcome Rejections

Faith will also help you to overcome rejections and failures. As you read in chapter four, I tried to start five businesses before my jewelry business succeeded. The others either failed or were just for a time and season. So what kept me going when things got tough?

I remember the experiences I had when I decided to test the waters and quit my corporate job in order to begin **Fantasy Wear.** I began to sell jewelry and clothing from my home. I was trying to decide how to launch out and begin my business when my mother told me to just take a leave of absence so that if things didn't work out I'd have something to go back to. I'm sure you've heard people say, "Don't burn your bridges because you might have to go back." Well, I want to tell you that when you leave corporate America you have to blow that bridge up! You don't want to have to go back. It's either sink or swim. However, because my mother was such a strong influence in my life, I couldn't tell her that I blew up my bridge and quit my job. She thought that I simply took a leave of absence.

So I began Fantasy Wear, a direct sales and marketing network that sold clothing and jewelry from my home. In my first month I sold $16,000 worth of merchandise. In the second month I did the same. As the money came in I began renovating my house, and my consultants saw how I was prospering. So they decided that even though they were getting paid, they weren't going to make me rich. By the third month I had lost the entire business.

Naturally, my mother said, "Go back and get that job honey." I had to tell her, "Mother, there isn't a job to go back and get." That was some serious stuff. I became depressed and gained about 30 to 40 pounds. Sometimes I couldn't even get out of bed— I didn't want to get out of bed. I didn't know what to do. All I could do was lay in the bed and pray. But like my friend Les Brown says, "If you can look up, you can get up!" And I did! One day I got out of that bed and started **Traci Lynn Fashion Jewelry**. It began from nothing to something.

You see, even though the business venture failed I did not think of myself as a failure. Yes I accepted the fact that the businesses failed, but it was that method that failed not me. So I started my business from my home again, but this time I did things differently. I only worked from my home for a short time; I had learned my lesson. I wrote down my goals. I wanted to have 50 consultants in two months and make a certain amount of money so that I could open up my showroom. I was out in the shops with a 50-tray case saying, "Would you like to buy some jewelry?" I did whatever I had to do. And do you know what happened? The very next year after I opened my showroom we came close to the million-dollar mark in sales. That earned me a television interview on *Good Morning America* for being a "Young Entrepreneur Under 30 Who Hit the Jackpot." It was faith that kept me during the hard times and helped me achieve my dream.

I always knew that I could succeed once I found the right business. Faith was a key when I wanted to get on at that radio station and the station manager kept telling me that he wasn't ready for that idea yet. I didn't take the rejection personally. You can't either. Life equals tough times. You will face some difficulties in life, but you have to know how to let them go and keep going. Forget the mistakes, bad experiences, and failures of the past. Look towards the future.   Don't hold grudges; they only hinder you.   Don't call up everyone you know and complain.That will only make the situation worse. Remember, you will have what you say, and you don't want to become a source of negative energy.   Stand in faith and keep going. Remember, if you're following God's vision for your life, all things are working together for your good.

Resist Negative Limitations

Faith will also help you to resist negative limitations. I was on a Canadian tour with a company that I speak for. And one of the speakers said to me, "You know, Traci, people like me and you, we'll never be big time speakers. We'll never be a Les Brown...so we have to be content where we are." Had I simply sat there and said nothing, I would have agreed with what he was saying. He would have placed his negative limitations on me and I would have quietly accepted it. I didn't though. My response was, "No, no, no! You're talking about you. You can't talk about me." You have to correct people when they say things like that. Don't allow them to put negative limitations on you. It's up to you to stand in faith and say, "No matter what it looks like, I'm *Coming Soon!*"

Walk in faith with each step you take. Remember, no matter what you encounter on the road to delivering your baby, everything is a stepping-stone. Take what you've learned at one step and apply it someplace else. Use that information and knowledge to catapult you to the next level. Before you know it you will have gone from one thing to another, then another, and another. Each step of faith will lead you to a new level.

Why Shouldn't I Be Rich?

"Beloved, I wish above all things that thou mayest prosper and be in health,even as thy soul prospereth" (3 John 2).

A lot of people don't think that they should be rich. They don't want a lot of money because they think that money is evil. The Bible doesn't say that *money* is evil. It says that the *love* of money is the root of all evil. If you were to lay a dollar bill on the floor it wouldn't move unless something else was moving it. Money can't lie, cheat, or steal. Only the master of the money can make it do those things; so money is not evil. It is the master of the money that is evil.

Money can be used to do a lot of good things too. You need money to finance your plans and get ahead. You need money in order to live in the house you want, and to pay for that car you've dreamed about owning. If you are going to finance your vision, you need money. Did you know that there is no shortage of money in this world? Millions of dollars are being hoarded by a few selfish people, but there is plenty money to go around.

The Purpose for Money

How can you finance your vision without money? The reason why you need to have money is so that you can walk in your vision. When you are living from paycheck to paycheck, it's hard to break loose from the job and start your own business. The job has become your life source, and it prevents you from fulfilling your vision. You can't let it go. So you hold on to it like a prostitute holds on to a pimp. Does your job treat you so well that it should have those rights to your life? You should have the money you need without feeling that you're going to die if you leave your job.

Dead Men Walking

On the other hand, a lot of people die because they can't leave their jobs. People have more heart attacks on Sunday night and Monday mornings than on any other days of the week. The reason why is because they go to jobs that make them sick. Their jobs make them sick because they are not fulfilling their purpose. Then there are others who are dead men walking. They go to work everyday, but they are dead. They died at the age of 21 but are waiting until they are 65 to be buried. That's because they failed to live their purpose in life. Instead of pursuing their passions, they worked on jobs and let their visions and dreams die. They're dead men walking, just waiting to take their visions to the grave.

Think about that for a minute. I have an Aunt Sarah who can bake and cook like you wouldn't believe. One Easter we ate dinner at her house, and I asked her why she never opened up a restaurant. She said, "Honey it takes money." I asked her if she would have done it if she had the money. She said, "Absolutely. It's my passion. It's my love." Unfortunately, some people never fulfill their passions.

How many people are letting something as small as money stop them from fulfilling their purpose? This is the land of abundance. You are kings and queens, ambassadors and peculiar people. God has already provided for you. You just need to ask Him for what you want. He wants you to fulfill your vision. So ask yourself again, "Why shouldn't I be rich?"

Often, people use the money they have unwisely. Take for instance the person who buys expensive cars when he or she doesn't even own a house yet. This person drives a Mercedes when he doesn't have a dime in the bank. He wants everybody to see his success, but what he's really showing everybody is that he can pay a car note. Now there is nothing wrong with owning luxury vehicles. It is important however, that you spend your money wisely. Make wise choices. After all, money is not attracted to people who have a lot of debt. Otherwise, your money will end up merely paying your debts, not fulfilling your vision. God designed you for a purpose and He wants you to accomplish it before you leave this earth.

I'm Not Finished Yet

If you knew that you only had twenty-four hours

left to live what would you get rid of in your life? A couple of months ago I was on an airplane returning from Atlanta to Philadelphia when my plane was struck by lightning. It was a large plane carrying two hundred and sixty-seven passengers. It kept going up and down, while tipping from side to side. People began screaming, "Ah, we're going to die!" And I heard a man say, "…We're all going to die because it's somebody else's time." That was an evil report. And I said, "No! I will live and not die! I've got books to write! I've got people to talk to!" The other people had gotten caught up in the circumstances. They had lost hope, but I know my purpose, and I have a vision.

When you find yourself in the storms of life, it is your vision that will make you say, "No, I've got things to do." You see, with a vision you will realize that you can't leave this earth until your purpose has been achieved. So seek God and discover your purpose. Pursue your vision and fulfill your destiny. As you do so you will find that it is possible to inherit the promises of God.

Inherit the Promises

"So do not throw away your confidence; it will be richly rewarded. You need to persevere so that when you have done the will of God, you will receive what he has promised"
(Hebrews 10:35,36; NIV).

My prayer is that this book has changed your life. I hope you have been transformed into a different person. I want you to view life differently now and realize that you are here for a purpose, and it's time to fulfill it. Once you connect to God—the power source—He will give you the anointing to achieve your purpose. As you diligently apply everything that you've learned from this book, you will find that you have everything you need to fulfill your destiny. The rest is up to you. Let's review the seven steps to completion.

The Tongue is a Creative Force

Till Your Own Land

Overcome Fear

Get Out of the Wilderness

You Are the Key

Faith

Why Shouldn't I Be Rich?

Begin today to bring out the millionaire inside of you. Implement these steps and you'll find yourself going places and doing things you'd only dreamed of doing. Step-by-step you will fulfill your divine design. So prepare to enjoy life and become everything that God intended for you to be. Don't allow situations and circumstances to dictate the course of your life any longer. Trust Him as you live each day by faith. And remember, you will win if you don't give up. For the race isn't given to the swift or the strong, but to the one who finishes.

Following are some positive affirmations. Encourage yourself as you begin to speak them regularly. Remember, you were born a winner; so you are destined to win. Live your dreams, and enjoy life to its fullest. You can become the millionaire God created you to be!

Positive Affirmations

I am different.

I'm set apart.

I'm peculiar.

I'm unique.

I'm wonderfully and fearfully made.

I was created for a purpose—a

divine purpose.

I was a winner from the womb. I won the race.

I have millionaire status on the inside of me.

All the pain, all the disgrace, and all the problems are behind me.

I won't look back. I'm a Millionaire in Motion

I'll look to the hills from which cometh my help.

My help, my anointing, my gift, and my power come from the Lord.

As of today I am changed.

I am transformed.

I am changed!

Products by Traci Lynn

Wealth Without Sorrow
(Book)

Activating Your Dreams
(3 tape series)

Mind of a Millionaire
(2 tape series)

Stress Buster
(3 tape series)

Power Leadership
Skills for Women
(4 tape series)

Birth Your Vision
(4 tape series) available on video

God's Plan for Prosperity
(3 tape series)

Stress Buster
(3 tape series)

Don't Break Down Break Through
(4 tape series)

Money with a Mission
(2 tape series) available on video